MAPS OF THE

GDS

The Garden of Eden & the ancient use of Earth's Tectonic Plates to

map the division of the Earth to Noah's sons

CARDELLI

MAPS OF THE GODS

Revised and Expanded Second Edition: July 2021

ISBN-13: 978-1-7371111-2-2

Printed in the United States of America

Contents

Introduction   v

Maps of the Gods   1

References   73

List of Figures   78

About the Author   81

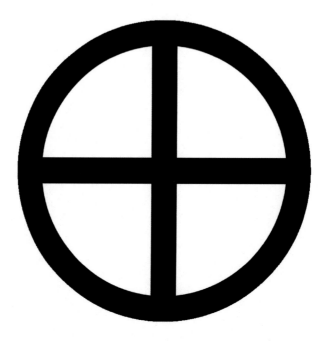

Introduction

I would never have considered myself an expert on history, much less religion or even mythology. Though the subjects have certainly intrigued me for so many years.

Neither do I consider my formal education as anything impressive. It consists of a bachelor's degree in Aeronautical Science from Embry-Riddle Aeronautical University. My master's degree, which I abandoned two courses shy of completion, was a specialization in Space Studies.

I place more value on the knowledge that comes from studying the many ancient history and ancient religious books that line the walls of my office.

My experiences and travels around the world during my two decades of military service have also contributed greatly to my perspectives.

For many committed Christians, faith is the only requirement that matters. For those of us who have studied the Bible and cannot get past all of the inconsistencies and conflicting stories, we find that we need more than faith, because there are so many questions. Even our most highly revered religious leaders in this day and age will freely admit how little the modern day Bible resembles its original translation.

Neither is it a secret that there are very few names, places, or events in the Bible that can be corroborated through other, separate historical records. Why?

I grew up southern Baptist, reading the New King James Bible. Throughout my Christian childhood, I always felt that something was off. As a lover of history, I have always wondered, why does the Bible jive so little with everything else? And why have we not found proof of the things that it says allegedly happened?

Likewise, I have always been fascinated by ancient mythology for as long as I can remember. Stories of gods and goddesses, of their incredible dwelling places and mystical powers.

These stories seemed like fun and imaginative fairy tales, which would be awesome if true, but of course we all knew were just myth. Still, I couldn't help but wonder if there was something out there that originally fed those mythologies, something that gave them rise, gave them fuel. One small fact that snowballed into a full-blown mythology. Could this perhaps have happened with some religions as well? Could it all be somehow tied together?

For most of my adult life I considered myself an agnostic, believing that a hitherto unknown great architect created us and our environment. However, I had not found a definitive answer on what His true identity was, at least to a point of satisfaction for me.

I believed there are truths in many of our ancient writings. Some of it certainly lost in translation over the millennia, but much of it still hidden in plain sight. I believe some of it to be tainted by the pre-conceived notions and biases of priests, kings and translators with their own agendas and radical views, and some of it not. But how can we discern truth from deception? It is my hope that this book is a start for those that are compelled to begin, or maybe continue on that daunting journey. To search for the facts, wherever they lie, and let them lead us wherever they may.

I approached the research and writing of Maps of the Gods from a different perspective than likely most people would. I started this project with no loyalty to any one religion, no bias towards any one version of history over another. I just started with a question.

During my many deployments and visits to foreign places, I was struck by the complexities and diversities of ancient cultures. By the sheer awesomeness of ancient structures that no one can really explain the origin of. I couldn't help but feel we were missing something, something that has been lost or forgotten in time. Something ancient that has been hidden, either unintentionally or perhaps intentionally. I felt that there had to be a universal truth that had not yet been discovered. A truth that ties together all our ancient mythologies, all our religions, all our superstitions, together into one defined concept.

Something that brings science, magic and spirituality all together into one defined truth. An explanation that is the truth behind the legends of giants, dwarves, and various races of humanoids, such as the "hobbit people" discovered in Indonesia not so long ago. A truth behind the abilities of clairvoyants, and those that can see and sense things the rest surely cannot. Perhaps in antiquity the doors between our world and another world, maybe a spiritual one, were wide open. Possibly with frequent travel between.

I wonder if these were the times I have read about in the book of Genesis. The account of fallen angels who allegedly mated with human women and produced the Giants, hybrid offspring that would undoubtedly have carried their DNA. Perhaps the Great Flood did not wipe out all the hybrid humans carrying their DNA, and to this day select humans in our population are periodically born with the characteristics of those beings, such as abilities of seeing entities from the other side, of being able to foresee future events, being able to put forth scientific theories well beyond the comprehension of the majority of the rest of the human race.

Perhaps there are genetic markers in the DNA of these people with those certain characteristics that can be identified and compared, to see if we can discern our human DNA from that of those fallen angels, the "Watchers", and their Nephilim progeny in an attempt to prove or disprove that theory. I was driven to find out more, and I had to start somewhere. An origin point.

My intention is not to try to disprove this belief system or prove that belief system. Neither is the intention to destroy anyone's faith or try to change a religion. I suspect the results of this work can be used by both sides to attack each other. The intention is only to stimulate discussion. To broach a sensitive subject, and any subject that approaches the subject of religion from a different angle is always hotly contested. No, my intention is to simply garner attention that perhaps our ancient history that we all comfortably believe to be accurate, may not be as accurate as we think. And perhaps there are buried truths in our current religions that we have not yet been made aware of. This book is the first step in my exploration of that belief. The first step of many to come.

Our presented history, to this day, has seemingly been guided and influenced by whatever the dominant religion, politics and powers were of the time. And there have been many, and perhaps that is why there are so many contradictions and puzzles in our past. However, maybe there is a 'pure' line of history with a pure origin, separate from the one recounted in our ancient history books that has deviated due to human influences. Maybe, if we can trace that history back to some point where it falls back on track, following the true story backed by facts, we will discover that Science, Religion and Mythology actually do tie together at points.

These factual points of connection are what I will only briefly refer to as my 'Conjunction Theory'. My suspicion of the existence of a deeply hidden coalescence of Science, Religion and Mythology that makes up the real truth of our reality, of our past. Perhaps then we can begin to clearly see what's behind the curtain. Maybe we really can have it all. Question is, would we really want it…

~ Cardelli

MAPS OF THE GODS

"We may never know for sure". Found within the pages of
any common household Bible is a description of the Garden of
Eden. But the Bible has underwent major transformation since its
earliest versions. In order to make it more reader friendly we now
have numerous versions, some of which barely compare to its
original form.

For this book I will reference the New King James Version
(NKJV) translation of the Bible's Old Testament, as my source for
scriptures in the book of Genesis.

Genesis 2:8 states: *"The Lord God planted a garden
eastward in Eden, and there He put the man whom He had
formed...10 Now a river went out of Eden to water the garden, and
from there it parted and became four riverheads. 11 The name of
the first is Pishon; it is the one which skirts the whole land of*

Havilah, where there is gold. 12 And the gold of that land is good. Bdellium and the onyx stone are there. 13 The name of the second river is Gihon; it is the one which goes around the whole land of Cush. 14 The name of the third river is Hiddekel; it is the one which goes toward the east of Assyria. The fourth river is the Euphrates." [1]

Note how Genesis 2:14 says, *"The name of the third river is Hiddekel."* Almost every other version of the Bible identifies the third river instead as the Tigris River. Why? Is the New King James Version translation of the river's names in Genesis correct? Yes or No? Why is the NKJV translation different from other versions of the Bible? Was one of the river names originally the "Hiddekel" River, and changed to the "Tigris" River?

Could it be possible that translators and priests, with their own bias and their own belief systems, changed "Hiddekel" to Tigris, because, maybe they felt they had a better idea of where certain places, like the Garden of Eden, should be located? Or should I maybe say "he", as in Wilhelm Gesenius, the man credited with interpreting "Hiddekel" as "the rapid Tigris"?

The aim of the 130 translators of the New King James Version translation project in 1975 was to adhere to "complete equivalence" principles of translation of the earliest known manuscripts, in contrast to the "readability" equivalence used by the contemporary translators in the original 1611 King James Version (KJV) translation. So, indeed, with the NKJV we find inconsistencies with not only the 1611 KJV, but most modern translations as well. Although a refreshing departure from the norm, that being said, it certainly gives me a warm and fuzzy feeling knowing we have such smart, unbiased individuals translating our most important works both in modern times and back in antiquity!

Many books, many websites, many theories have been put forth on the subject of the Garden of Eden. Some theories with such sketchy references and ideas as to be ridiculous that it was even published in the first place. In the end, authors may very well end their claim with something like, "*although we may just never know for sure*". Ok, if even *you* are not totally convinced, then why bother publicizing that theory?

There are theories that have placed the Garden of Eden in Iraq, some in Ethiopia, others in Egypt and still others in the Americas. Many based on flimsy scraps of obscure ancient references that in some cases were possibly made up, with little of substance or fact to back it up. Let us take the popular theory of the Garden of Eden's location in Iraq. This theory is based on the idea that two of the four branches of the rivers described in Genesis are the Tigris and Euphrates. So they trace the mouth of those two rivers back to southern Iraq and, voila! There's the Garden of Eden! Hmmm....really? That desolate patch of sand was the most wondrous place on Earth?

Certainly much has changed since antiquity. The landmarks, the water levels, and surely the names can at times be completely different, or borrowed from other locations. Geographical features have changed, and bodies of water have formed, and also dried up. And much has been lost in translation undoubtedly. As a result, I have always felt the true key to finding the lost location of the Garden of Eden was not in the identification of the four branch river system itself, but rather encrypted in the correct division of the lands for Noah's sons. So it goes to say, without a true and correct map of the division of the lands, the Garden would never give up its location. So I resolved myself to remedy that.

The Book of Jubilees

For many years, the Book of Jubilees was suspected to be a modern writing, or possibly an inaccurate translation at the least. An original, ancient source could not be produced. When was the book originally written? By whom? A valid question, until the discovery of the Dead Sea Scrolls. There, fragments of the book were discovered, and after comparison with current examples, proved the writings were accurate and consistent with the current version. Suddenly the authenticity of the book was accepted. So now the Book of Jubilees is widely accepted as an authentic text from antiquity, likely written around 100-200 BCE.

The Book of Jubilees has also been referred to as the Book of Division, since within its pages the infamous division of the Earth to Noah's sons Shem, Ham, and Japhet is recounted.

In the Book of Jubilees the account of the division of the Earth to Noah's three sons is exhaustingly detailed. It uses names of places that in many cases cannot be validated or located in modern times. So, throughout history it is likely many names were simply attributed to locations that fit the preconceived notions of whoever was commenting on it, with only the slightest of true geographical reference.

The result was numerous versions of maps of the division referenced for hundreds, if not thousands of years which are still to this day peddled as fact. A typical representation is Figure 1.

We can see in Figure 1 the "division of the earth", which seems to barely only cover a portion of the Middle East.

For me, if I was Noah, and the world was just divided and given to my sons, I would feel robbed. What? Is that all? Where is the rest of our land?

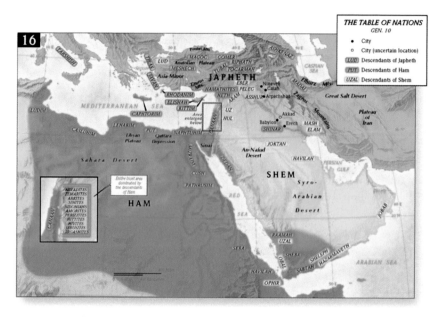

Figure 1. Typical Map of Shem, Ham and Japhet Lands

These maps have been created using the same reference points for centuries, for example, using the Tigris River as the main reference or origin point.

Why has no one ever bothered to question the validity of the acceptance of the Tigris River as the main reference point in almost EVERYTHING? Take away the Tigris River, and suddenly everyone goes back to square one. Which is a problem.

Few may be aware that the Book of Jubilees does not just divide the land up to Shem, Ham and Japhet. It further divides the land up to all *their* sons, Noah's grandsons. It goes into minute

6

detail describing lands and islands in the sea, and various other specific geographical features.

Many "maps" of the portions for Shem, Ham and Japhet exist out in the public domain, but it does not seem anyone has ever attempted to try to explain the further division of the earth to the grandsons.

So then why was all that explicit detail put into the description, if none of it was to be taken seriously, or accepted as fact?

It stands to reason that the ancients were talking about real land boundaries, real physical features and real places. *Important ones.* But how can we figure it all out as it relates to the all-important Tigris River?

Well, just for fun, moving forward we will remove the Tigris River from any and all reference points. From now on, we will continue as if the Tigris River is simply just another part of the Euphrates River system, and a hitherto unknown river named the Hiddekel is in fact the third river. That could be controversial.

Naturally, that is where we will choose to start.

The Division Amongst Noah's Sons

So, get your hands on a World Map and let us begin.

The passages I will be referencing are from the Book of Jubilees translated from the Ethiopic by Reverend George Henry Schodde and published in 1888.

Ok, so here we go. The division amongst Noah's sons.

The narrative of the division can be found in Chapter VIII starting with verse 8. The entire division narrative is as follows:

Chapter VIII, verse 8 – "And it happened in the beginning of the thirty-third jubilee, and they divided the earth into three parts, to Shem and to Ham, and to Japhet, each one his inheritance, in the first year of the first week, while an angel, one of us who were sent to them, was there.

9. And he called his sons, and they came to him, they and their children, and he divided the earth by lot what his three sons should take, and they stretched out their hands and took to themselves the writing out of the bosom of their father Noah.

10. And there came out on the writing as the lot for Shem the middle of the earth, which he and his children should have as an inheritance for the generations unto eternity, from the middle of the mountain Râfû, from the exit of the water of the river Tinâ, and

his portion goes toward the west through the midst of this river,
and they go until they approach the abyss of the waters out of
which comes this river, and this river empties and pours its waters
into the sea Miôt, and this river goes into the great sea: all that is
toward the north of this is Japhet's, and all that is to the direction
of the south is Shem's.

11. And it reaches until it comes to Karâsô, which is in the
bosom of the tongue which looks toward the south.

12. And his portion reaches unto the great sea, and reaches
straight until it approaches the west of the tongue which looks
toward the south; for the sea is called the tongue of the Egyptian
sea.

13. And it turns from there toward the south, toward the
mouth of the great sea in the shore of the waters and proceeds
toward Arabia and Ophrâ, and it proceeds until it reaches to the
water of the river Gejôn and toward the south of the water of
Gejôn, along the shore of this same river.

14. And it proceeds toward the north until it approaches
the garden of Eden, toward the south thereof to the south, and from
the east of the whole land of Eden, and toward the whole east, and
it turns to the east, and proceeds until it approaches toward the
east of the hills whose name is Râfâ, and it descends toward the
border of the outlet of the water of the river Tinâ.

15. This portion came out in the lot for Shem and his sons, and he remembered his word which he had spoken with his mouth in prophecy, for he had said: 'Blessed be the Lord God of Shem, and may the Lord dwell in the dwelling of Shem!'

17. And he knew that the garden of Eden is the holy of holies, and the dwelling of the Lord, and Mount Sinai, the centre of the desert, and Mount Zion, the centre of the navel of the earth, these three, opposite one another, were created as sanctuaries.

18. And he blessed the God of gods who had put the speech of the Lord into his mouth.

19. And he knew that a blessed portion and a blessing had come to Shem and to the children of his generations forever, the whole land of Edom, and all the land of the Erythrian sea, and all the land of the east, and India and at the Erythrian and the mountains thereof, and all the land of Bâsôr, and all the land of Lebanon and the islands of Kuphatûr, and all the land of Elâm and Asûr and Bâbêl and Sûsân and Mâdâr, and all the mountains of Ararat, and all the land beyond the sea which is beyond the hills of Asûr toward the north, a blessed and prosperous land, and all that is in it is very good.

20. And for Ham came out as the second portion, beyond the Gijôn, toward the south, to the right of the garden, and it proceeds to all the fire mountains, and goes toward the west to the sea Atil, and goes to the west until it reaches to the sea of Mâûk, of that one into which everything descends that is destroyed.

21. And it proceeds to the north to the shore of Gâdil and goes to the west of the water of the sea until it approaches the river Gejôn, and the river Gejôn goes until I approaches to the right of the garden of Eden and this is the land which came forth for Ham as the portion he shall retain for himself and the children of his generations forever.

22 And for Japhet there came forth a third portion beyond the river Tinâ toward the north of the exit of its waters, and it goes toward the northeast the whole district of Lâg and all the east thereof.

23. And it goes toward the north to the north and goes to the mountains of Kilt, toward the north and toward the sea Mâuk and it goes toward the east of Gadir over toward the coast of the water of the sea.

24. And it proceeds until it approaches the west of Para, and returns toward Aphêrâg, and goes toward the east, towards the waters of the sea Meât. And it goes toward the shore of the river Tinâ, toward the east of the north, until it approaches to the shore of the waters thereof, toward the mountain Râfâ, and it bends toward the north.

25. This is the land which came forth for Japhet and his children as the portion of his inheritance which he should hold unto eternity for himself and the children of their generation unto eternity five great islands and a great land in the north, only it is cold, but the land of Ham it is hot, and the land of Shem has neither heat nor frost, for it mixed in coldness and heat." [2]

The Division Amongst the Sons of Shem, Ham and Japhet

Chapter IX continues the narrative by detailing the individual inheritances to each of Noah's grandsons.

Chapter IX, verse 1 - "And Ham divided among his sons, and the first portion came out for Ques toward the east, and to the west of him for Phud, and to the west of him for Kainan toward the west of the sea.

2. And Shem also divided among his sons, and the first portion came forth for Elam and his sons toward the east of the river Tiger, until it approaches the east, the whole land of India and on the Erythrian and its coast, and the waters of Dêdan and all the mountains of Mêbri and Ela, and all the land of Sûsan, and all that is on the side of the Phêrnak to the Erythrian sea and the river Tina.

3. But for Asûr came forth a second portion, all the land of Asûr and Nineva and Sinaôr and to the border of India, and ascends along the river.

4. And for Arphaksed came forth a third portion, all the land of the district of the Chaldees toward the east of the Euphrates, bordering on the Erythrian sea, and all the waters of the desert until near to the tongue of the sea which looks toward Egypt, and all the sand of Lebanon and Sanêr and Amana to the border of the Euphrates.

5. And for Aram came forth as a fourth portion all the land of Mesopotamia, between the Tiger and the Euphrates, toward the north of the Chaldees, to the border of the mountains of Asur.

6. And the land of Arara came out as fifth portion to his son, the mountains of Asur and all belonging to them until it reaches to the east of Asur, his brother.

7. And Japhet, too, divided the land of his inheritance between his sons, and the first portion came forth for Gômêr toward the east, from the north side to the river Tina. And in the north there came out for Magog all the inner portions of the north until reaches the sea Mêat.

8. And for Madai came forth as his portion that he should possess, to the west of this two brothers, unto the islands and unto the coasts of the islands. And the Egawan came forth as a fourth portion all the islands, and the islands which are toward Edalûd.

9. And for Tôbêl came forth as a fifth portion, between the tongue which approaches toward the side of the portion of Lûd, to the second tongue, unto beyond the second tongue into the third tongue.

10. And for Melek came forth as a sixth portion, all that beyond the third tongue, until it approaches to the east of Gadir.

11. And for Tiras came forth a seventh portion; four great islands in the midst of the sea, which approach to the portion of Ham, and the islands of Kamatûra came out for the sons of Arphaksed in his division of his inheritance by lot.

12. And thus the sons of Noah divided out to their children, in the presence of Noah their father, and he caused them to swear an oath cursing him who endeavored to seize a portion which had not been allotted him. " [3]

Shem's Inheritance

Let us begin with Shem's portion: *"And there came out on the writing as the lot for Shem the middle of the earth, which he and his children should have as an inheritance for the generations*

14

*unto eternity, from the middle of the mountain Râfû, from the exit
of the water of the river Tinâ, and his portion goes toward the west
through the midst of this river, and they go until they approach the
abyss of the waters out of which comes this river, and this river
empties and pours its waters into the sea Miôt, and this river goes
into the great sea: all that is toward the north of this is Japhet's,
and all that is to the direction of the south is Shem's.*

*11. And it reaches until it comes to Karâsô, which is in the
bosom of the tongue which looks toward the south.*

*12. And his portion reaches unto the great sea, and reaches
straight until it approaches the west of the tongue which looks
toward the south; for the sea is called the tongue of the Egyptian
sea.*

*13. And it turns from there toward the south, toward the
mouth of the great sea in the shore of the waters and proceeds
toward Arabia and Ophrâ, and it proceeds until it reaches to the
water of the river Gejôn and toward the south of the water of
Gejôn, along the shore of this same river.*

*14. And it proceeds toward the north until it approaches
the garden of Eden, toward the south thereof to the south, and from
the east of the whole land of Eden, and toward the whole east, and
it turns to the east, and proceeds until it approaches toward the*

east of the hills whose name is Râfâ, and it descends toward the border of the outlet of the water of the river Tinâ." [4]

We have to start somewhere. Until now, the going consensus has always been to use the Zagros Mountains as the aforementioned "Mountain Rafa", though I can find no source or reason for why anyone should use this as the reference point. That is, other than referencing the Tigris River that flows in its region.

Well, since I have stated that we will no longer be referencing the Tigris, then that no longer works. Besides, I'm thinking bigger. We are talking about the division of the WORLD. I need to be looking for BIG mountains. After all, a common translation for "Rafa" is "giant". I am trying to find large features of the Earth as reference points. In addition, Shem supposedly gets India in his portion, right?

Indeed, the Book of Jubilees 8:19 confirms: *"And he knew that a blessed portion and a blessing had come to Shem and to the children of his generations forever, the whole land of Edom, and all the land of the Erythrian sea, and all the land of the east, and India and at the Erythrian and the mountains thereof,"* [5]

To stay true to the description we, at a minimum, must start east of India. What is east of India?

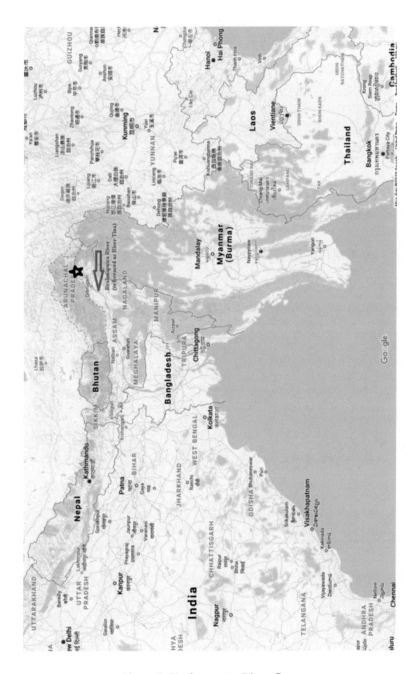

Figure 2. Brahmaputra River flow

Referencing Google Maps, we find the Himalayan mountain range. And what river is exiting right out of the middle of it? The Brahmaputra River.

In Figure 2, we can see that it comes down from the middle of the Himalayan Mountains, and flows west and then down into the Bay of Bengal. The Bay of Bengal then opens into the Indian Ocean. This looks like it may just be our starting point.

Let us continue going piece by piece through the description: *"from the middle of the mountain Râfû, from the exit of the water of the river Tinâ, and his portion goes toward the west through the midst of this river, and they go until they approach the abyss of the waters out of which comes this river, and this river empties and pours its waters into the sea Miôt, and this river goes into the great sea"* [6]

It makes sense that the "river Tina" is the present-day Brahmaputra River. We can easily follow the Brahmaputra River to the west, through its "midst", and down into the Bay of Bengal.

Searching through an assortment of National Geographic maps, I pull out a map of the Indian Ocean Floor.

In Figure 3, one can clearly see just off the coast what is known as the Ganges Cone. It's a significant drop off which goes straight into the Ceylon Abyssal Plain. A legitimate, aptly named "abyss".

Figure 3. Ganges Cone and Ceylon Abyssal Plain

The reference to the "sea of Miôt" must be to the present-day Bay of Bengal. The "great sea" that it flows into must be the present-day Indian Ocean.

Continuing on: *"all that is toward the north of this is Japhet's, and all that is to the direction of the south is Shem's."* [7]

Using my new reference point, this tells me that the Himalayan mountain range is the northern boundary, with everything north of it belonging to Japhet, and everything south belonging to Shem. This works great, because now Shem gets India!

Next, *"And it reaches until it comes to Karâsô, which is in the bosom of the tongue which looks toward the south.*

12. And his portion reaches unto the great sea, and reaches straight until it approaches the west of the tongue which looks toward the south; for the sea is called the tongue of the Egyptian sea." [8]

From the outlet of the waters of the river, we can draw a line to the southernmost tip of India, which not surprisingly, looks like a tongue pointing to the south. It would seem that "Karaso" might actually be Sri Lanka located just off the coast. Perhaps this is what is meant by "in the bosom of the tongue". However, at this point we will refrain from using Sri Lanka as the actual reference point and just stick with the southern tip of India, the "tongue".

So, from there we can draw a straight vector line west to the southern tip of the Arabian Peninsula. Again, that part looks like a tongue pointing south. And not surprisingly, the sea right next to it is the Red Sea, otherwise called the Egyptian Sea. This is great, we are still matching up.

Next, *"And it turns from there toward the south, toward the mouth of the great sea in the shore of the waters and proceeds toward Arabia and Ophrâ, and it proceeds until it reaches to the water of the river Gejôn and toward the south of the water of Gejôn, along the shore of this same river."* [9]

We then orient ourselves facing south and cross the channel to the shore, and from there head west to the "river Gejôn" or "Gijon". My suspicion is that the river Gijon is what is historically known as the Nile River. The source of the Nile River is Lake Victoria with the shores of the river in Uganda. Using this as my new landmark we arrive at the beginning of the Nile River above Lake Victoria.

Next, *"And it proceeds toward the north until it approaches the garden of Eden, toward the south thereof to the south, and from the east of the whole land of Eden, and toward the whole east, and it turns to the east, and proceeds until it*

21

approaches toward the east of the hills whose name is Râfâ, and it descends toward the border of the outlet of the water of the river Tinâ. " [10]

Now we follow the Nile River north somewhere, and according to the description this supposedly approaches the Garden of Eden. There the Garden of Eden is used as a geographical reference point, but without knowing exactly where the Garden is, we are now at a dead end.

All we can do at this point is continue our mapping with the portion allotted to Ham.

Book of Jubilees 8:20 - "And for Ham came out as the second portion, beyond the Gijôn, toward the south, to the right of the garden, and it proceeds to all the fire mountains, and goes toward the west to the sea Atil, and goes to the west until it reaches to the sea of Mâûk, of that one into which everything descends that is destroyed.

21. And it proceeds to the north to the shore of Gâdil and goes to the west of the water of the sea until it approaches the river Gejôn, and the river Gejôn goes until I approaches to the right of the garden of Eden and this is the land which came forth for Ham as the portion he shall retain for himself and the children of his generations forever. " [11]

Here we have geographical names and points that match nothing in our historical record. If we assume that "beyond the Gijon, toward the south" is where we left off with Shem's portion, then that means we are proceeding to the south of Africa. We would then travel west to the sea, and then further west into another sea.

If Africa belongs to Ham, it would seem so does the South Atlantic, and perhaps South America.

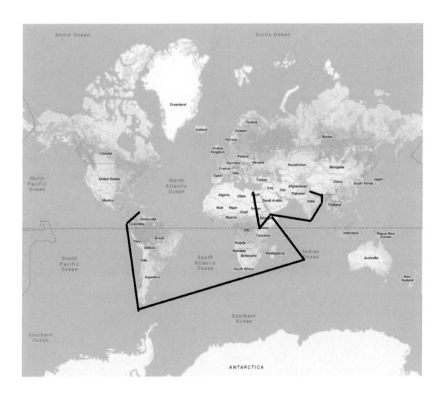

Figure 4. Initial rough plotting of Shem and Ham lands

In order to see if we can find further verification, we must look into these "fire mountains".

These "fire mountains" sound like volcanos to me. To see if there are any volcanos in southern Africa, we will google a Tectonic Activity map. Here is where we make a startling discovery.

Printing out the Tectonic Plate map and comparing it to the map where we have been crudely drawing our boundary lines for Shem and Ham, we can see that *it is nearly identical.*

Comparing Figure 4 with Figure 5, one can see that without knowing it, we have been roughly following tectonic plate lines.

Our boundary lines for Shem and Ham are following tectonic plate lines, eerily matching nearly every point.

With this new revelation, we can switch over to an Earth Tectonic Plate map, and start over with our original reference point, the Himalayan Mountains.

This time we will use the tectonic lines as our boundary lines.

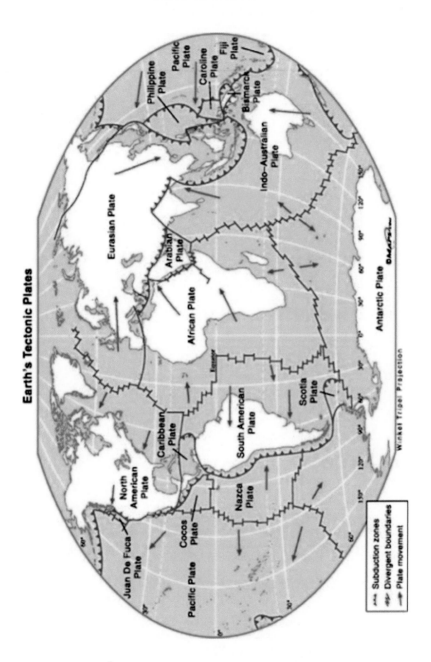

Figure 5. Earth's Tectonic Plate Map

Right off the bat one notices there is no tectonic line following the river or reaching towards the southern tip of India.

Neither is there one forming a straight line from India to the southern point of the Arabian Peninsula. However, that is where the inconsistencies end. So, before finishing Shem's portion of land, we will map out Ham's portion as it is written, now referencing a tectonic map for our guidelines.

Whereas Shem's portion is very precisely detailed with points, Ham's portion seems a little more directional. Perhaps because this is because Shem's portion deviates from tectonic lines at two points, whereas Ham's portion mostly just follows the tectonic lines.

Once again using the Nile River as our Gijon River reference, moving toward the south, we start where we previously left off with Shem's portion, toward the south of the Gijon River at Lake Victoria.

Next, *"And for Ham came out as the second portion, beyond the Gijôn, toward the south, to the right of the garden, and it proceeds to all the fire mountains,"* [12]

We proceed to all the "fire mountains" from there. This must be referencing ALL of the "fire mountains", including those located off of Africa's shore. Africa's volcanoes extend out into

26

the Indian Ocean, with the farthest one located south in the Reunion Islands (Piton De La Fournaise). This means we are now following the Somalian Plate tectonic line.

Next, *"...and goes toward the west to the sea Atil,"* [13]

I believe the sea of Atil is the present-day Atlantic Ocean, and we can follow the Southwest Ocean Ridge line west.

Next, *"...and goes to the west until it reaches to the sea of Mâûk of that one into which everything descends that is destroyed."* [14]

Let us assume the sea of Mâûk is the present-day Pacific Ocean, which means Ham gets South America as part of his portion, all the way to the west coast where the Pacific Ocean starts.

Referencing the tectonic plate map, it is also at this exact location where the Nazca Plate subduction zone is located, a logical explanation for "into which everything descends that is destroyed".

Next, *"it proceeds to the north to the shore of Gâdil"* [15]

Let us assume "Gâdil" to be present-day North America, and we follow the subduction zone to its end at a point at the western coast of Central Mexico. Let us keep this point in mind for future reference.

Next, *"and goes to the west of the water of the sea until it approaches the river Gejôn"* [16]

To the west of the water seems a little unclear. We can follow the Caribbean Plate tectonic line from the western coast of central Mexico to the east to the Mid-Atlantic ridge tectonic line, but that goes *through* the water, not around or west of the water. Also, we cannot follow the tectonic lines all the way to the Nile if we stay west of the water and run north along the North American east coast.

That is when I realized that the ancients must have been using a second mapping system. The first, Earth's Tectonic Plate map, and the second, a Global Ocean Current map. Referencing a Global Ocean Current map, we can see in Figure 6 that we can now follow to the "west of the water of the sea", onto the Gulf Stream which carries us northwest to the North Atlantic Current. Then onto the Canary Current which carries us right to the Straits of Gibraltar, on the way to the Nile.

Coming off the Canary Current, where do we go now?

Next, *"and the river Gejôn goes until it approaches to the right of the garden of Eden: and this is the land which came forth for Ham as the portion he shall retain for himself and the children of his generations forever."* [17]

It was here that I hit another brick wall in my research. The Garden of Eden is already being referenced, and we have not arrived anywhere near the Nile yet. I went back to the description of Shem's portion, when I was still at Lake Victoria.

"And it proceeds toward the north until it approaches the Garden of Eden, toward the south thereof to the south, and from the east of the whole land of Eden," [18]

It was while trying to work out the Gijon River/Garden of Eden relationship that I had a stunning revelation.

The River of Gijon is not just the Nile River. The River of Gijon at one time was the present-day Mediterranean Sea. Its mouth was the Straits of Gibraltar. The Nile was actually just a branch off of it.

The Mediterranean Sea considered a river?

Over millennia the Mediterranean water levels have risen significantly. In some estimates as much as 120 meters over the last 14,000 years, submerging ancient coastal cities ever since. The ancient city of Heracleion was just recently discovered at the bottom.

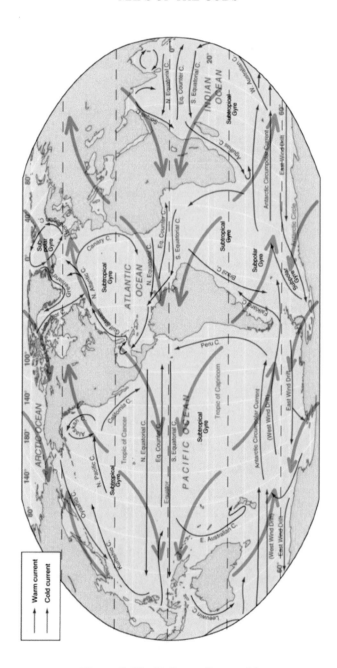

Figure 6. World Ocean Current Map

Using this radical new perspective, we are now getting close to figuring out the location of the Land of Eden and pinpointing the location of the Garden of Eden.

Since we are possibly in the vicinity of the Garden, let us take a break from mapping out the rest of the lands and try to locate the Land of Eden instead. First, however, we have to locate the other three river branches described in the Book of Genesis.

The Four Rivers

Genesis 2:10 states: *"Now a river went out of Eden to water the garden, and from there it parted and became four riverheads. 11 The name of the first is Pī'shon; it is the one which encompasses the whole land of Hav'ilah, where there is gold. 12 And the gold of that land is good. Bdellium and the onyx stone are there."* [19]

We know that with climate change, various seasons and weather patterns, water levels rise and fall and rivers swell and recede and in some cases may even merge together.

In order to identify the first river, the Pishon River, I believe the key is in its description. Let us assume for now that Gihon in Genesis is Gijon/Gejon in the Book of Jubilees and the Gihon branch of the river is the Nile, which runs south, and that

31

the Euphrates really is the Euphrates, which is way out east. So let's go with what we know.

"The name of the second river is Gī'hon; it is the one which goes around the whole land of Cush." [20]

If today's Mediterranean was the River of Gihon flowing east in the past, and is now the current-day Nile, then this description fits perfectly. The Gihon flows from the Mediterranean south into Ethiopia.

As seen in Figure 7, roughly halfway through Sudan the Nile splits into the White Nile and the Blue Nile. What does the Nile now encircle? It encircles the area of the ancient land of Cush, which is now current-day Sudan and Ethiopia.

"The fourth river is the Euphrates." [21]

Looking at Google Earth maps, a clear path from the source of the Euphrates to the Mediterranean Sea is visible with small lakes and rivers with an outlet into the Mediterranean northwest of Cypress.

It is with that connection that I believe the Euphrates is the fourth river.

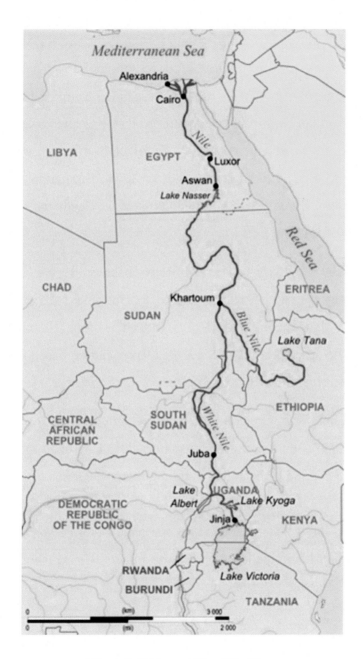

Figure 7. White and Blue Nile River

All of this leaves little room for the Pishon River, which is described as encircling a whole land, so let's look toward the North. The empire of Attila the Hun descended from the 108 clans of the Scythian Nation. At various times they occupied vast areas including Persia and areas north of the Black Sea that is now western Russia, including the area of Moscow. Hungarian Chronicles tell that at one point the King of the Scythians "entered the land of Havilah". [22]

Could the "land of Havilah" have been used interchangeably with Scythian land in ancient times? A river encircles Moscow, the River Volga. Indeed, ancient settlements around the upper courses of the Volga River can be traced back to the ancient Scythians and Huns.

I believe at one point the Volga River connected to the current Black Sea, through the Bosphorus strait, through the sea of Marmora and the Aegean Sea to the Mediterranean Sea or, River of Gihon. I believe as the Gihon "flowed" east it made a sharp turn north into the Aegean Sea and thus starts the River Pishon. The Volga River being the latter part of the ancient River Pishon. With that, we have the first branch.

"The name of the third river is Hiddekel; it is the one which goes toward the east of Assyria." [23]

34

As I have previously stated, I do not accept that the Hiddekel is the Tigris. However, I do believe the description to be correct. In order for this river to fit, it must meet two data points.

First, the river must connect to the Mediterranean, and second it must flow toward an eastern Assyrian border. As a result, I believe this river to be the Jordan River.

The Assyrian empire underwent numerous territorial transitions over its long history. Without knowing at which time we are referencing the Assyrian empire's boundaries, one cannot reference any one map of Assyria.

However, for our purposes, can we find a time period that does work for the Jordan River?

The ancient Neo-Assyrians were located in and around the area currently referred to as the Fertile Crescent. In Figure 8 we see a typical map of the Fertile Crescent.

In Figure 9 we see a typical map of the Neo-Assyrian Empire occupying the Fertile Crescent area.

If we use the Jordan River as our third river, we suddenly see how the Jordan River flows towards an eastern boundary of the Assyrian territory.

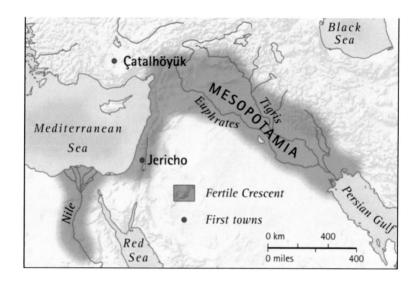

Figure 8. Fertile Crescent

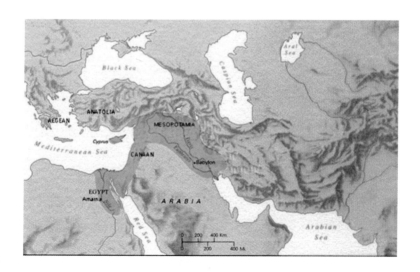

Figure 9. Neo-Assyrian empire ca. 670 BCE

Interestingly, the peak of the Neo-Assyrian Empire around 670 BCE coincides closely with the time period many modern scholars believe the authorship of Genesis took place, around the 6th century BCE.

I believe there was a point in antiquity where the Jordan River connected to the Mediterranean through the area of present-day Lebanon. The Jordan River feeds thru the Dead Sea, which has salinity levels similar to that of ocean water. Perhaps the high salinity levels result from a period when the Mediterranean fed ocean water into and thru it via the Jordan River.

A connection to the Mediterranean, with its flow in relation to the time period of the Neo-Assyrian Empire, makes the third river fit the description perfectly. Interestingly, the Jordan is referenced in Genesis 13:10 and states: *"And Lot lifted his eyes and saw all the plain of Jordan, that it was well watered everywhere (before the LORD destroyed Sodom and Gomorrah) like the garden of the LORD, like the land of Egypt as you go toward Zoar."* [24]

Jordan was watered like the garden of the Lord? I believe this to be a reference that the River Jordan was once known as part of the river system that watered the Garden of Eden.

Using this new four-branch river system as our map, we can now map out the flow of the River of Eden. Assuming an aerial view, if the mouth of the River of Gijon is at the Straits of Gibraltar, the river flows east and eventually divides into four heads.

The first is the Volga River which heads north through to the Black Sea and encircles present-day Moscow.

The second river, turns at Egypt and runs south as the present-day Nile and encircles present-day Ethiopia.

The third goes straight through present-day Lebanon and flows south as the Jordan River along the border of Syria and through the Dead Sea.

The fourth river is the Euphrates that connected through present-day southern Turkey.

With the River Gijon charted, we should now be able to locate the Land of Eden.

Using the reference in Ham's description that the Gijon River runs to the right of the Garden of Eden:

"and the river Gejôn goes until it approaches to the right of the garden of Eden: and this is the land which came forth for Ham as the portion he shall retain for himself and the children of his generations forever." [25]

Using the reference in Shem's description that the Gijon River runs to the south of the Land of Eden:

"And it proceeds toward the north until it approaches the Garden of Eden, toward the south thereof to the south, and from the east of the whole land of Eden," [26]

We can now determine that the Land of Eden is southern Europe as seen in Figure 10. Since the river "waters" the Garden of Eden prior to dividing into four branches, that means the Garden of Eden lies along the LEFT of the river somewhere between the Straits of Gibraltar and Egypt, in the east of the Land of Eden.

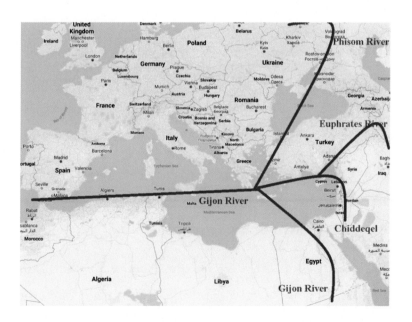

Figure 10. Mediterranean Sea as River Gijon with 4 branches

The Garden of Eden

Three parts relate to the location of the Garden, the first and second parts are in the description of Ham's portion. At the beginning of Ham's mapping:

"And for Ham came out as the second portion, beyond the Gijôn, toward the south, to the right of the garden," [27]

The second part, at the end of the mapping of Ham's lands when we arrived at the straits of Gibraltar:

"and goes to the west of the water of the sea until it approaches the river Gejôn, and the river Gejôn goes until it approaches to the right of the garden of Eden..." [28]

Now that we have a new perspective on the river Gijon, we can finish mapping out Ham's portion utilizing the ocean currents and tectonic lines and then use that map as a reference to assist us in pinpointing the Garden of Eden.

We need to reference the third part that relates to the location of the Garden of Eden in the description of Shem's portion, where we were at Lake Victoria:

"And it proceeds toward the north until it approaches the Garden of Eden, toward the south thereof to the south, and from the east of the whole land of Eden," [29]

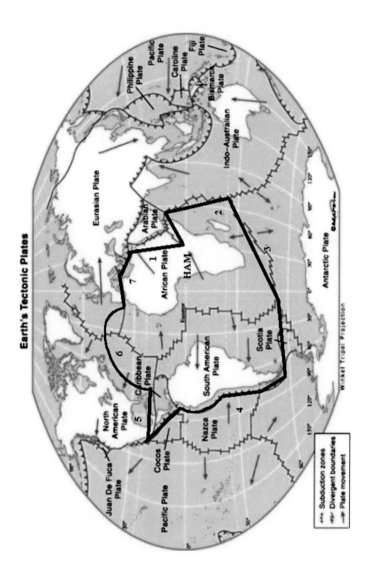

Figure 11. Tectonic Map showing Ham's Land following: 1. Gijon River, 2.

Boundary of Somalian Plate and Southwest Indian Ocean Ridge, 3. Nazca

Subduction Zone, 4. Caribbean Plate, 5. Gulf Stream, 6. North Atlantic Current,

Canary Current, 7. Gijon River

41

This pinpoints the exact location of the Garden. If we follow the Gijon east and the Nile north we end up in one region, Greece. The Garden of Eden therefore lies in Greece. Furthermore, I believe that Athens is the geographical center of the Garden of Eden.

Before we complete mapping Shem's portion, let us see if everything we know about the Garden of Eden in Genesis correlates with its new location.

"The Lord God planted a garden eastward in Eden." [30]

I have determined that southern Europe is the Land of Eden, and Greece is obviously located to the east. So Yes.

"Now a river went out of Eden to water the garden, and from there it parted and became four riverheads." [31]

The river Gijon "flows" east below southern Europe to and around Greece and splits into four branches. Yes.

Another description can be found in the Book of Jubilees 8:17: *"And he knew that the garden of Eden is the holy of holies, and the dwelling of the Lord, and Mount Sinai, the centre of the desert, and Mount Zion, the centre of the navel of the earth, these three, opposite one another, were created as sanctuaries."* [32]

Opposite one another I take to otherwise mean facing each other. Let us triangulate it and see if that makes sense.

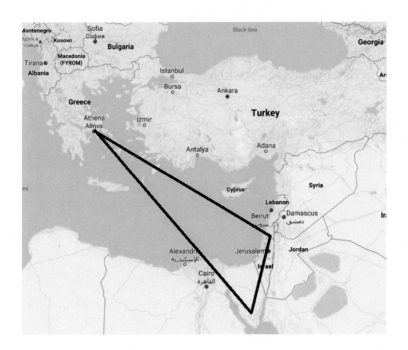

Figure 12. The Three Holy Sites

As seen in Figure 12, it would appear that they are definitely facing each other. So another yes.

Genesis 3:24 states: *"So He drove out the man; and He placed cherubim at the east of the garden of Eden, and a flaming sword which turned every way, to guard the way to the tree of life."* [33]

Wait, what? Cherubs with a fiery sword? Ok, if we make the "fiery sword equals volcanoes" assumption then we need to look for volcanoes.

In Figure 13, surrounding Athens we clearly see the South Aegean Volcanic Arc. Fiery swords turning about. Cherubs guarding the way. So yes.

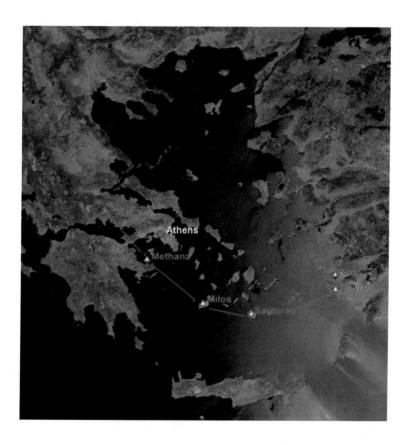

Figure 13. South Aegean Volcanic Arc

This brings us to an interesting question. If Greece, specifically Athens, is the true location of the Garden of Eden, does this form a direct connection between the Holy Bible and ancient Greek Mythology?

Interestingly, during my naval service, one of my deployments took me sailing on a ship through the Straits of Gibraltar. For this event, I earned a crossing certificate inducting me into the "Order of the Rock". In Naval service, sailors receive certificates for crossing or serving in a handful of specially recognized places around the world. Ancient seafarers have observed some of these ceremonies for centuries. The Order of the Rock is a ceremonial designation for one's sailing through the "Pillars of Hercules" into the mystic wonders of the land beyond.

Some of us thought it was a little over the top for something that seemed a bit trivial. However, if the Pillars of Hercules truly was the entrance from the sea into the Land of Eden, that certificate may become my new favorite.

What about the Garden's location being described as located east in the Land of Eden? Taking into account our new interpretation of the Mediterranean being the river Gijon, Shem's lower portion now follows along the lower Eurasian Tectonic line through the Mediterranean and out the Straits of Gibraltar. But how far east and north does the Land of Eden go?

In order to precisely answer that question, we must finish mapping the lands of Shem. Now that we know the Mediterranean Sea is the river Gijon and the Straits of Gibraltar is the mouth, we can continue the mapping of Shem's Land.

"And it proceeds toward the north until it approaches the Garden of Eden, toward the south thereof to the south, and from the east of the whole land of Eden," [34]

Referencing back to Figure 10, we simply follow the river.

"and from the east of the whole land of Eden, and toward the whole east, and it turns to the east, and proceeds until it approaches toward the east of the hills whose name is Râfâ, and it descends toward the border of the outlet of the water of the river Tinâ." [35]

I previously stated that I believe the Land of Eden is southern Europe, if that is true, then that would describe Shem's portion as including much of Europe, and from its westernmost boundary to the east all the way back to the Himalayas, as indicated in Figure 14.

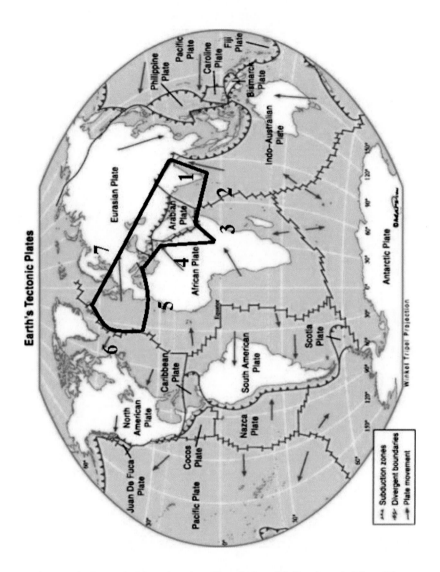

Figure 14. Tectonic Map showing Shem's Land following: 1. River Tina

(Brahmaputra) southwest vector, 2. West vector, 3. Volcanic Rift line, 4. Gijon

River, 5. Eurasian Plate Tectonic Line, 6. Mid-Atlantic Ridge Tectonic Line, 7.

East Eurasian Plate Tectonic Line, River Tina (Brahmaputra)

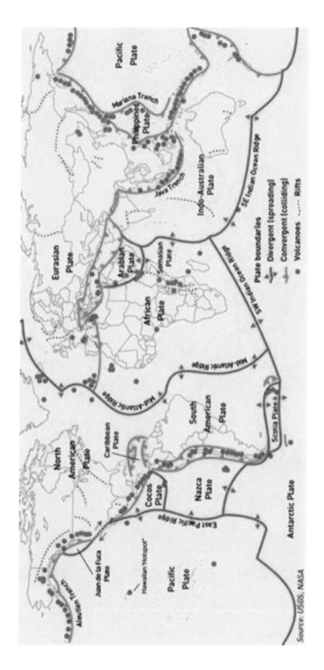

Figure 15. Tectonic Convergence Lines

However, how far north does Shem's land portion go?

Referencing Figure 15, the Northern Convergence runs from the Himalayas in a line straight towards the British Isles. For now, let us assume the British Isles as the northwest boundary, and all of Shem's portion includes everything east of it up to the Northern Convergence, and back to the Himalayas. We will see if we can pinpoint the northwest boundary of Shem's portion more accurately during the mapping of Japhet's portion.

Since Japhet is essentially left with the remainder of the world, there is less detail and more directional information. Also, we can no longer use two dimensional mapping. We will need to use a globe, because on a two dimensional map "north" is just straight up. On a globe, however, north can be either northeast or northwest as it points toward the top of the Earth.

Now we reach for a globe to assist us as we continue to follow the directions.

Book of Jubilees 8:22 - "And for Japhet there came forth a third portion beyond the river Tinâ, toward the north of the exit of its waters, and it goes toward the northeast the whole district of Lâg, and all the east thereof. 23. And it goes toward the north to the north, and goes to the mountains of Kilt, toward the north and toward the sea Mâûk, and it goes toward the east of Gadir over toward the coast of the water of the sea. 24. And it proceeds until it

49

approaches the west of Para, and returns toward Aphêrâg, and goes toward the east, towards the waters of the sea Mêat. And it goes toward the shore of the river Tina, toward the east of the north, until it approaches to the shore of the waters thereof, toward the mountain Râfâ, and it bends toward the north." [36]

We start at the exit of the Brahmaputra River into the Bay of Bengal and move northeast.

I believe the translation should read north *and* east. As in everything north, as well as everything east. Japhet is getting the remainder of the world, so we are getting general directions, while rarely mentioning specific places only when necessary.

If we reference a globe, and follow the 90 degree longitude line that passes through that region, we can map everything east along that arc. This includes Indonesia and Malaysia and all the islands. It also includes Vietnam, Cambodia, and Laos - which I believe to be the district of Lag - and EVERYTHING east, including Australia and onward.

"And it goes toward the north to the north, and goes to the mountains of Kilt," [37]

Remember, we are in directional mode now, so north to the north is telling me we are heading to the top of the world. We are following longitudinal lines as well as also reaching out somewhere to the mountains of "Kilt" as a reference point.

I believe "Kilt" is a reference to "Celt", and I believe this is a clear reference to the mountainous present-day British Isles as a western reference point. And if so, we just got solid verification for the northwest boundary of Shem's portion exactly where we expected it to be.

"toward the north" [38]

Still holding that globe? From the mountains of Kilt we go straight north to the top of the world. We are still going north so keep spinning that globe down...

"and toward the sea Mâûk," [39]

Through the Bering Strait we go and into, yes, the Pacific Ocean. Or, as I referenced earlier, what I believe to be the sea of Mâûk.

"and it goes toward the east of Gadir over toward the coast of the water of the sea." [40]

I believe Japhet owns the whole sea of Mâûk, and as we continue to spin the globe moving through the Pacific Ocean we end up at Antarctica. And as I have pointed out, I believe Gadir is South America.

Here we once again pick up tectonic lines and ocean currents for our final ride home. And I do mean ride, since I believe the South Atlantic/Antarctic Currents are the "coast of the water of the sea" that is being referenced, which will begin east of the southern tip of South America or "Gadir".

"And it proceeds until it approaches the west of Para, and returns toward Aphêrâg" [41]

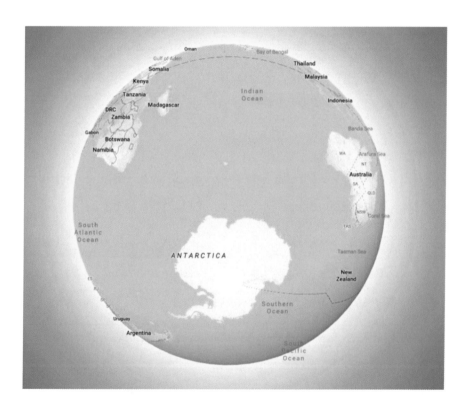

Figure 16. Globe orientation after passing through Sea of Mâûk

If you were holding your globe and spinning it the whole time as I was, following the Pacific Ocean down to South America, your globe should now be oriented like mine as seen in Figure 16.

I believe Aphêrâg is current day Africa and Para is current day Antarctica. Interestingly, a quick check on Google shows Para is a root that can mean "Beyond". Could "Para" at one point also have been called "Fara", or "Far" as in "Far Land"?

Continuing on, as one can see in Figure 16, South America (Gadir) is now situated to the left, and Antarctica to the right. Proceeding to the west of Antarctica (Para) we move along the east coast of South America (Gadir) and pick up the South Atlantic/Antarctic Currents and tectonic line towards Africa. This puts us right under Ham's portion, riding under and along the Southwest Indian Ocean ridge heading east.

"and goes toward the east, towards the waters of the sea Mêat." [42]

We continue to follow the tectonic line until we are at the southeast corner of Ham's portion, in sighting distance of the Bay of Bengal, or the Sea of Mêat.

"And it goes toward the shore of the river Tina, toward the east of the north, until it approaches to the shore of the waters [43] *thereof, toward the mountain Râfâ, and it bends toward the north."*

53

On to the final leg. To the east of the north, staying under Shem's portion, straight into the Bay of Bengal.

Then I remembered noticing something a while back. Referring back to Figure 3 again, I could see the etching of the ocean floor in the Ganges Cone directly below the Brahmaputra River.

Looks like we have an actual point on the shore to follow "east of the north" to the Brahmaputra River and up to the Himalayan range.

It was then that I realized, there must have been a fourth map they were using as a reference. A map of the World's Ocean Floors.

Wait a minute, so now even the world's ocean floors were already mapped? Did SONAR exist back then?

And how did they know about that "abyss", anyway?

Regardless, this completes our map of Japhet's lands as depicted in Figure 17.

Ok, let us see if our map matches what the Book of Jubilees says that Japhet ended up with.

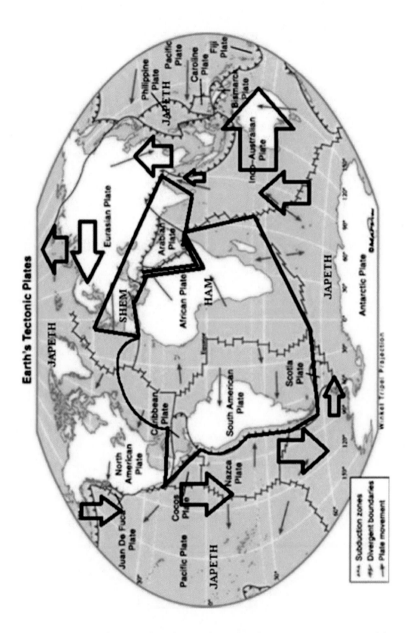

Figure 17. Tectonic Map showing Japhet's land, encompassing everything

outside of Shem and Ham portions

Book of Jubilees 8:25 states: *"This is the land which came forth for Japhet and his children as the portion of his inheritance which he should hold unto eternity for himself and the children of their generation unto eternity: five great islands and a great land in the north; only it is cold, but the land of Ham it hot, and the land of Shem has neither heat nor frost, for it mixed in coldness and heat."* [44]

I believe that the "great land in the north" is the bulk of Asia, and I believe the five great islands to be North America, Greenland, Australia, Antarctica, and Papua New Guinea. Many of which are cold regions. Ham got Africa and South America, which is hot.

Shem got the land from Western Europe to India, which is neither hot nor snowy, mixed in coldness and heat.

It is also clear that the only way to follow the description of the division of Japhet's portion is to follow it across a circular model of the Earth. So the only conclusion is, this partitioning of the Earth that was described in a book written over two thousand years ago, was being directed and observed...*from space.*

This would indicate, at a minimum, the necessity of a non-terrestrial presence during those proceedings.

Book of Jubilees 8:8 states: *"And it happened in the beginning of the thirty-third jubilee, and they divided the earth into three parts, to Shem and to Ham, and to Japhet, each one his inheritance, in the first year of the first week, while an angel, one of us who were sent to them, was there."* [45]

Who was this "angel"? How much influence did this angel contribute to the discussion and decision of the division?

Continuing on, let us see how Shem's portion matches up. Noah seemed pretty happy with it.

Book of Jubilees 8:19 states: *"And he knew that a blessed portion and a blessing had come to Shem and to the children of his generations forever; the whole land of Edom, and all the land of the Erythrian sea, and all the land of the east, and India and at the Erythrian and the mountains thereof, and all the land of Bâsôr, and all the land of Lebanon and the islands of Kuphatûr, and all the land of Elâm and Asûr and Bâbêl and Sûsân and Mâdâr, and all the mountains of Ararat, and all the land beyond the sea which is beyond the hills of Asûr toward the north, a blessed and prosperous land, and all that is in it is very good."* [46]

Referencing our map of Shem's portion in Figure 14, Shem gets the Erythrian Sea (Persian Gulf), all the land of the east, India, the Himalayas, Lebanon, the land of Iraq and Syria and the

57

mountains of Ararat, and the whole Land of Eden (southern Europe), as well as all three Holy Sites.

Yes Noah, it is indeed *very* good.

Division Amongst Noah's Grandsons

Now that we have mapped out the division of the Earth among Shem, Ham and Japhet, and used that division to locate both the Land of Eden and the Garden of Eden, we can now tackle the hard part. The further division of the lands amongst the sons of Shem, Ham and Japhet.

The Book of Jubilees goes into great detail with the portioning out of the lands, and I can imagine many readers over time probably just glossed over it as nonsense because it did not fit their preconceived notion that all the apportioned land should be located smack in the middle of the Middle East.

As far as I am concerned, this further subdivision has always been the ultimate test of the accuracy of my conclusions. If the further division of the lands to the grandsons are compatible with world geographical features and what I have already mapped out, then we get to a point where there is just too much corroboration for it to be coincidence or blind luck.

For this mapping, we again have to reference a globe of the Earth to understand it clearly.

Division Amongst Ham's Sons

Book of Jubilees 9:1 states: *"And Ham divided among his sons; and the first portion came out for Ques toward the east, and to the west of him for Phud, and to the west of him for Kainan toward the west of the sea."* [47]

Referencing Figure 17, our new map of the division of the Earth to Noah's sons, we can now figure out what lands were apportioned to the grandsons. Since Ham got Africa and South America, his three sons split those two continents. In looking at the traditionally accepted division of lands, Ham only had eastern Africa. But of course I have apportioned all of Africa to him. The land of Canaan, now in present-day Israel, is towards the east of Africa, not in Ham's portion, and definitely not to the west of any sea. The Book of Jubilees explains why this is.

Book of Jubilees 10:22 states: *"And Ham and his sons went into the land which he had taken, which fell to him by lot in the land of the north [south]; and Kainaan saw the land of the Libanon to the canal of Egypt that it was very good, and he did not go into the land of his inheritance to the west of the sea, and dwelt in the land of Libanon to the east and to the west of the land of the Jordan and on the coast of the sea. 23. And Ham, his father, and Cush and Mêzrêm, his brothers, said to him: 'Thou hast settled in a land which is not thine and did not fair to us by lot, thou shouldst not do thus; for if thou doest thus, then thou and thy children will fall by condemnation in the land, and as cursed ones by sedition, for by sedition ye have settled and by sedition thy children will fall and thou wilt be rooted out to eternity. 24. Do not dwell in the dwelling place of Shem, for to Shem and his children was it given by lot. 25. Cursed art thou and cursed shalt thou be above all the sons of Noah by the curse which we covenanted with an oath between is in the presence of the holy judge and before Noah our father.' 26. But he did not listen to them and dwelt in the land of Libanon from Emath to the entrance of Egypt, he and his sons until this day. 27. And on this account this land is called Canaan."* [48]

Interesting that the angel present during the apportioning is referred to as a "holy judge".

I believe the account of Kainaan moving north to settle in Canaan to be accurate. Since Kainaan moved out of Ham territory, his two brothers are left with both continents to themselves.

I believe that Phud settled around the central part of Africa, and Ques (or Cush) to the east, and I believe since Kainaan was not interested in South America, Ques also headed out to the west of the sea. Earlier I stated the northwestern point of Ham's territory was the western coast of Central Mexico.

If we look into Mesoamerican Culture, specifically the Aztecs, they worshipped a deity there named Quetzalcoatl. This deity is represented as a winged serpent and was a teacher of knowledge. I believe Ham's son Ques could very well be the mythical Quetzalcoatl, possibly arriving postdiluvian and teaching the indigenous people there.

Division Amongst Japhet's Sons

Japhet had many sons, as well as a lot of territory. Is it possible for all the territories to be portioned out and still match the descriptions? That is, with nothing left over, and nothing missing? Let us see if it is even possible.

Book of Jubilees 9:7 - "and the first portion came forth for Gomer toward the east, from the north side to the river Tina." [49]

Gomer- Central Russia, Western China, Nepal.

"And in the north there came out for Magog all the inner portions of the north until it reaches the sea Mêat." [50]

Magog - Eastern Russia, Eastern China, Mongolia, Burma, Thailand, Vietnam.

"And for Madai came forth as his portion that he should possess, to the west of his two brothers, unto the islands and unto the coasts of the islands." [51]

Madai - (Northern) Europe, Western Russia, Kazakhstan, Iceland, Islands in Arctic.

"And to Egawan came forth as a fourth portion all the islands, and the islands which are toward Edalûd." [52]

Egawan - I believe Edalûd to be Taiwan. So those would be the Philippines, Indonesia.

"And for Tôbêl came forth as a fifth portion, between the tongue which approaches toward the side of the portion of Lûd, to the second tongue, unto beyond the second tongue into the third tongue." [53]

Tobel - I believe Lûd to be Eastern China and the tongue which approaches to be South Korea. This would make the three portions Japan, Petropavlovsk Peninsula and beyond to Alaska as shown in Figure 18.

"And for Melek came forth as a sixth portion, all that beyond the third tongue, until it approaches to the east of Gadir." [54]

Melek – If we reference Figure 17, we can see this to be the remainder of North America.

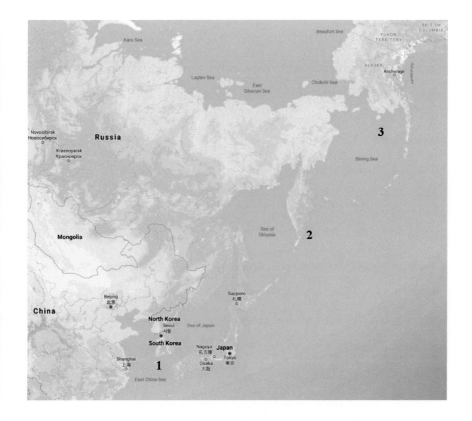

Figure 18. The Three Tongues

"And for Tiras came forth a seventh portion; four great islands in the midst of the sea, which approach to the portion of Ham." [55]

Tiras - New Zealand, Antarctica, Australia, Tasmania.

"and the islands of Kamatûra came out for the sons of Arphaksed in his division of his inheritance by lot." [56]

63

Arphaksad's sons - Papua New Guinea and eastern islands.

Clearly, as I have assigned them, the lands are more or less balanced, with desirability and distance away obviously playing a part in their size. But more importantly, *everything fits.*

Division Amongst Shem's Sons

Book of Jubilees 9:2 states: *"And Shem also divided among his sons, and the first portion came forth for Elam and his sons toward the east of the river Tiger, until it approaches the east, the whole land of India and on the Erythrian and its coast, and the waters of Dêdan and all the mountains of Mêbri and Ela, and all the land of Sûsan, and all that is on the side of the Phêrnak to the Erythrian Sea and the river Tina. 3. But for Asûr came forth a second portion, all the land of Asûr and Nineva and Sinaôr and to the border of India, and ascends along the river. 4. And for Arphaksed came forth a third portion, all the land of the district of the Chaldees toward the east of the Euphrates, bordering on the Erythrian sea, and all the waters of the desert until near to the tongue of the sea which looks toward Egypt, and all the sand of Libanon and Sanêr and Amana to the border of the Euphrates. 5. And for Aram came forth as a fourth portion all the land of Mesopotamia, between the Tiger and the Euphrates, toward the north of the Chaldees, to the border of the mountains of Asur. 6.*

64

And the land of Arara came out as a fifth portion to his son, the mountains of Asur and all belonging to them until it reaches to the east of Asur, his brother." [57]

The division of land for Shem's sons is all happening for the most part in the middle of one land mass, with many names of places having changed, some of which lost throughout time. However, if we stick to geographical features, we can at least identify anything that does not match up.

"and the first portion came forth for Elam and his sons toward the east of the river Tiger, until it approaches the east, the whole land of India and on the Erythrian and its coast, and the waters of Dedan and all the mountains of Mêbri and Ela, and all the land of Sûsan, and all that is on the side of the Phêrnak to the Erythrian sea and the river Tina." [58]

Any land located east of the river "Tiger" is going to be the same whether they are referencing the current Tigris River or the Jordan River. So we will go with the land of India, Erythrian Sea and its coast. This would indicate they are describing the land of eastern Pakistan and all of India, from the east side of the Indus River to the Brahmaputra River and down to the Gulf of Oman (part of Erythrean Sea).

65

I believe the land of Susan was a portion of Eastern Europe, along with the mountains of Mêbri and Ela, which I believe included the Alps and Carpathian Mountains.

"But for Asûr came forth a second portion, all the land of Asûr and Nineva and Sinaôr and to the border of India, and ascends along the river." [59]

Asur and Nineva are well-documented sites, and I believe Sinaor is a lost location closer to India.

"And for Arphaksed came forth a third portion, all the land of the district of the Chaldees toward the east of the Euphrates, bordering on the Erythrian sea, and all the waters of the desert until near to the tongue of the sea which looks toward Egypt, and all the sand of Lebanon and Sanêr and Amana to the border of the Euphrates" [60]

The Chaldeans are also well-documented and this matches their known settlements in Iraq, from the Persian Gulf up along the Euphrates.

All the waters of the desert until near the tongue of the sea which looks toward Egypt I believe references the Arabian Sea at the south-west portion of Shem's land (remember the straight line from the southern tip of India?) and the Egyptian Sea which is the present Red Sea. This land extends north to the border of the Euphrates beyond Saudi Arabia, Jordan and Syria.

I believe Sanêr and Amana are locations in Eastern Europe, as the Chaldean Empire is known to have extended into Europe.

"And for Aram came forth as a fourth portion all the land of Mesopotamia, between the Tiger and the Euphrates, toward the north of the Chaldees, to the border of the mountains of Asur." [61]

Mesopotamia is also well-documented, and seems to be described accurately here. Note how well northern Mesopotamia fits if we place it between the Euphrates and Jordan River instead of the "Tiger".

"And the land of Arara came out as a fifth portion to his son, the mountains of Asur and all belonging to them until it reaches to the east of Asur, his brother." [62]

I believe Arara to be Northern Turkey and the Ukraine regions.

Without modern geographical reference points, and armed only with ancient names many of which were lost long ago in antiquity, all we can do is verify that the regions that we do know about all fall within the lands of Shem, and without conflict with other regions of lands belonging to Ham or Japhet.

We can now say with sufficient certainty that no known lands conflicted with each other in their descriptions.

However, I do not believe that in the event of an inconsistency within the subdivision that we should then throw out the baby with the bathwater.

The reason I tackled the subdivision of the grandsons was to make a critical point. That point being, that the description of the division is so accurate relative to the various modern mapping systems we just used, that even when we delve into the minutia of the grandson's allocations that most of history has readily ignored, the territories can all still fit.

What are the odds of accomplishing that by mere chance?

The Maps of the Gods

Critics stubbornly sticking to their "traditional" views may gleefully search for a discrepancy here or there, but one simple fact remains. An account of the description of the partitioning of the Earth to the sons and grandsons of Noah, described in the Book of Jubilees, a book widely accepted to have been *written* at least two thousand years ago, has now been proven to be accurate with a near 100% match for our modern geography.

I emphasize the written part, because the account was of an event that allegedly took place much longer before, perhaps centuries, perhaps millennia prior to the writing of the Book of Jubilees.

The most incredible realization of it all is that in order to achieve that level of fidelity of the division described, we had to use four highly technical, modern mapping systems to detect it.

The first, a map of Earth's Tectonic Plates. The second, a map of the World's Ocean Currents. The third, a map of the World's Ocean Floors. And the fourth, a manufactured globe of the Earth. All resources and technologies which are not known to have existed two thousand years ago.

If the account in the Book of Jubilees is indeed factual, many staggering revelations become apparent. That means that the Earth was known to be "round" much earlier than thought. It proves that the Americas were "discovered" centuries earlier than has been taught.

What does it mean if Ham's son Cush or Ques was actually Quetzalcoatl, the powerful god worshipped by the Aztec civilization? If so, what gods of other civilizations can we now trace back to this division?

What does it mean if two millennia ago not only the Americas were already known to peoples in Europe and the Middle East, but travel to and from was routine? How can we explain that Antarctica, and every single island of any substantial size across our planet was not only known, but mapped as well?

Could this finally be proof that a worldwide civilization flourished tens of thousands of years ago?

Just how is it that ocean floors, subterranean features, subduction zones, volcanoes and tectonic plates across the planet were already known and mapped?

Discovering the origin point for our map to be at the Brahmaputra River gives us yet another revelation. Noah's Ark would not have come to rest on Mount Ararat as previously thought; it would have come to rest *in the Himalayan Mountains*.

How does finally pinpointing the true location of the Garden of Eden to Athens affect the world's current religions?

Could we actually be at a juncture where Science, Religion and Mythology are starting to blend together into a single new truth? What other mythologies will be found to show more truth than fiction? Perhaps most important of all, how does it all fit together?

If Noah and his descendants dispersed from India, does this indicate an origin of western religions in Indian mythology?

I believe this book is only the beginning. Perhaps other "maps" exist in the stars, in the compositions of the elements, in our weather patterns, and in our DNA, that point to an engineered design. But engineered by whom?

I believe a door has been opened and now all those searching for the hidden truth must pass through and begin their journey to discover all the maps of the gods, the tools that were used to design us, our environment, and even our reality, long ago in a forgotten time.

There are many mysteries left to be solved, but without a firm starting point based in fact, based in science. My intention for this book is to be a starting point. For this book to be a key that opens the door to lost and hidden knowledge, and the explanations that might reside behind it.

It is my hope that *Maps of the Gods* opens the reader's eyes to the realization that maybe we know much less than we thought of our true history, that what populates our school books and taught to our children may be pure conjecture, some of which has been twisted by zealots over the centuries attempting to sway their own followers. Perhaps it is time to question the truth of *every* book, regardless of where it leads us.

71

The vicious cycle of the sanitization of our true history must come to a halt, and we must look with fresh, uninfluenced eyes to our past. We must search with a new perspective not influenced by outdated school books and biased religious leaders and current politics. We must start at the beginning, taking into account everything we discover, that which fits history and that which does not.

Instead of filing abnormalities away in dusty storage rooms in the recesses of museums, or even worse destroying them, we must bring them all to light and let the world's brightest minds seriously analyze them in their entirety. Only then can we start to understand what our true origins are and what our destiny will come to be.

However, we must also be fully prepared and ready to accept a truth that leads us somewhere many of us may never have expected…

References

[1] The Holy Bible, New King James Version; Thomas Nelson, Inc.; 1992; Genesis 2:9-14; page 2

[2] Schodde, Rev. George H. (1888). *The Book of Jubilees, translated from the Ethiopic*, E.J. Goodrich; Chapter VIII, Verses 8-25; page 31

[3] Schodde, Rev. George H. (1888). *The Book of Jubilees, translated from the Ethiopic*, E.J. Goodrich; Chapter IX, Verses 1-12; page 33

[4] Schodde, Rev. George H. (1888). The Book of Jubilees, translated from the Ethiopic, E.J. Goodrich; Chapter VIII, Verses 10-14; page 31

[5] Schodde, Rev. George H. (1888). The Book of Jubilees, translated from the Ethiopic, E.J. Goodrich; Chapter 8, Verse 19; page 32

[6] Schodde, Rev. George H. (1888). The Book of Jubilees, translated from the Ethiopic, E.J. Goodrich; Chapter 8, Verse 10; page 31

[7] Schodde, Rev. George H. (1888). The Book of Jubilees, translated from the Ethiopic, E.J. Goodrich; Chapter 8, Verse 10; page 31

[8] Schodde, Rev. George H. (1888). The Book of Jubilees, translated from the Ethiopic, E.J. Goodrich; Chapter 8, Verses 11-12; page 31

[9] Schodde, Rev. George H. (1888). The Book of Jubilees, translated from the Ethiopic, E.J. Goodrich; Chapter 8, Verse 13; page 31

[10] Schodde, Rev. George H. (1888). The Book of Jubilees, translated from the Ethiopic, E.J. Goodrich; Chapter 8, Verse 14; page 31

[11] Schodde, Rev. George H. (1888). The Book of Jubilees, translated from the Ethiopic, E.J. Goodrich; Chapter 8, Verses 21-22; page 32

[12] Schodde, Rev. George H. (1888). The Book of Jubilees, translated from the Ethiopic, E.J. Goodrich; Chapter 8, Verse 20; page 32

[13] Schodde, Rev. George H. (1888). The Book of Jubilees, translated from the Ethiopic, E.J. Goodrich; Chapter 8, Verse 20; page 32

[14] Schodde, Rev. George H. (1888). The Book of Jubilees, translated from the Ethiopic, E.J. Goodrich; Chapter 8, Verse 20; page 32

[15] Schodde, Rev. George H. (1888). The Book of Jubilees, translated from the Ethiopic, E.J. Goodrich; Chapter 8, Verse 21; page 32

[16] Schodde, Rev. George H. (1888). The Book of Jubilees, translated from the Ethiopic, E.J. Goodrich; Chapter 8, Verse 21; page 32

[17] Schodde, Rev. George H. (1888). The Book of Jubilees, translated from the Ethiopic, E.J. Goodrich; Chapter 8, Verse 21; page 32

[18] Schodde, Rev. George H. (1888). The Book of Jubilees, translated from the Ethiopic, E.J. Goodrich; Chapter 8, Verse 14; page 31

[19] The Holy Bible, New King James Version; Thomas Nelson, Inc.; 1992; Genesis 2:10-12; page 3

[20] The Holy Bible, New King James Version; Thomas Nelson, Inc.; 1992; Genesis 2:13; page 3

[21] The Holy Bible, New King James Version; Thomas Nelson, Inc.; 1992; Genesis 2:14; page 3

[22] Korde, Zoltan. (1994). *Encyclopedia of the Early Hungarian History.*

[23] The Holy Bible, New King James Version; Thomas Nelson, Inc.; 1992; Genesis 2:14; page 3

[24] The Holy Bible, New King James Version; Thomas Nelson, Inc.; 1992; Genesis 13:10; page 16

[25] Schodde, Rev. George H. (1888). The Book of Jubilees, translated from the Ethiopic, E.J. Goodrich; Chapter 8, Verse 21; page 32

[26] Schodde, Rev. George H. (1888). The Book of Jubilees, translated from the Ethiopic, E.J. Goodrich; Chapter 8, Verse 14; page 31

[27] Schodde, Rev. George H. (1888). The Book of Jubilees, translated from the Ethiopic, E.J. Goodrich; Chapter 8, Verse 20; page 32

[28] Schodde, Rev. George H. (1888). The Book of Jubilees, translated from the Ethiopic, E.J. Goodrich; Chapter 8, Verse 21; page 32

[29] Schodde, Rev. George H. (1888). The Book of Jubilees, translated from the Ethiopic, E.J. Goodrich; Chapter 8, Verse 14; page 31

[30] The Holy Bible, New King James Version; Thomas Nelson, Inc.; 1992; Genesis 2:8; page 3

[31] The Holy Bible, New King James Version; Thomas Nelson, Inc.; 1992; Genesis 2:10; page 3

[32] Schodde, Rev. George H. (1888). The Book of Jubilees, translated from the Ethiopic, E.J. Goodrich; Chapter 8, Verse 17; page 32

[33] The Holy Bible, New King James Version; Thomas Nelson, Inc.; 1992; Genesis 3:24; page 5

[34] Schodde, Rev. George H. (1888). The Book of Jubilees, translated from the Ethiopic, E.J. Goodrich; Chapter 8, Verse 14; page 31

[35] Schodde, Rev. George H. (1888). The Book of Jubilees, translated from the Ethiopic, E.J. Goodrich; Chapter 8, Verse 14; page 31

[36] Schodde, Rev. George H. (1888). The Book of Jubilees, translated from the Ethiopic, E.J. Goodrich; Chapter 8, Verse 22; page 32

[37] Schodde, Rev. George H. (1888). The Book of Jubilees, translated from the Ethiopic, E.J. Goodrich; Chapter 8, Verse 23; page 33

[38] Schodde, Rev. George H. (1888). The Book of Jubilees, translated from the Ethiopic, E.J. Goodrich; Chapter 8, Verse 23; page 33

[39] Schodde, Rev. George H. (1888). The Book of Jubilees, translated from the Ethiopic, E.J. Goodrich; Chapter 8, Verse 23; page 33

[40] Schodde, Rev. George H. (1888). The Book of Jubilees, translated from the Ethiopic, E.J. Goodrich; Chapter 8, Verse 23; page 33

[41] Schodde, Rev. George H. (1888). The Book of Jubilees, translated from the Ethiopic, E.J. Goodrich; Chapter 8, Verse 24; page 33

[42] Schodde, Rev. George H. (1888). The Book of Jubilees, translated from the Ethiopic, E.J. Goodrich; Chapter 8, Verse 24; page 33

[43] Schodde, Rev. George H. (1888). The Book of Jubilees, translated from the Ethiopic, E.J. Goodrich; Chapter 8, Verse 24; page 33

[44] Schodde, Rev. George H. (1888). The Book of Jubilees, translated from the Ethiopic, E.J. Goodrich; Chapter 8, Verse 25; page 33

[45] Schodde, Rev. George H. (1888). The Book of Jubilees, translated from the Ethiopic, E.J. Goodrich; Chapter 8, Verse 8; page 30

[46] Schodde, Rev. George H. (1888). The Book of Jubilees, translated from the Ethiopic, E.J. Goodrich; Chapter 8, Verse 19; page 32

[47] Schodde, Rev. George H. (1888). The Book of Jubilees, translated from the Ethiopic, E.J. Goodrich; Chapter 9, Verse 1; page 33

[48] Schodde, Rev. George H. (1888). The Book of Jubilees, translated from the Ethiopic, E.J. Goodrich; Chapter 10, Verse 22-27; page 37

[49] Schodde, Rev. George H. (1888). The Book of Jubilees, translated from the Ethiopic, E.J. Goodrich; Chapter 9, Verse 7; page 34

[50] Schodde, Rev. George H. (1888). The Book of Jubilees, translated from the Ethiopic, E.J. Goodrich; Chapter 9, Verse 7; page 34

[51] Schodde, Rev. George H. (1888). The Book of Jubilees, translated from the Ethiopic, E.J. Goodrich; Chapter 9, Verse 8; page 34

[52] Schodde, Rev. George H. (1888). The Book of Jubilees, translated from the Ethiopic, E.J. Goodrich; Chapter 9, Verse 8; page 34

[53] Schodde, Rev. George H. (1888). The Book of Jubilees, translated from the Ethiopic, E.J. Goodrich; Chapter 9, Verse 9; page 34

[54] Schodde, Rev. George H. (1888). The Book of Jubilees, translated from the Ethiopic, E.J. Goodrich; Chapter 9, Verse 10; page 34

[55] Schodde, Rev. George H. (1888). The Book of Jubilees, translated from the Ethiopic, E.J. Goodrich; Chapter 9, Verse 11; page 34

[56] Schodde, Rev. George H. (1888). The Book of Jubilees, translated from the Ethiopic, E.J. Goodrich; Chapter 9, Verse 11; page 34

[57] Schodde, Rev. George H. (1888). The Book of Jubilees, translated from the Ethiopic, E.J. Goodrich; Chapter 9, Verse 2; page 33

[58] Schodde, Rev. George H. (1888). The Book of Jubilees, translated from the Ethiopic, E.J. Goodrich; Chapter 9, Verse 2; page 33

[59] Schodde, Rev. George H. (1888). The Book of Jubilees, translated from the Ethiopic, E.J. Goodrich; Chapter 9, Verse 3; page 33

[60] Schodde, Rev. George H. (1888). The Book of Jubilees, translated from the Ethiopic, E.J. Goodrich; Chapter 9, Verse 4; page 33

[61] Schodde, Rev. George H. (1888). The Book of Jubilees, translated from the Ethiopic, E.J. Goodrich; Chapter 9, Verse 5; page 34

[62] Schodde, Rev. George H. (1888). The Book of Jubilees, translated from the Ethiopic, E.J. Goodrich; Chapter 9, Verse 6; page 34

List of Figures

Fig. 1   Typical Map of Shem, Ham and Japhet Lands   Page 6

Source: http://catholicheartbeatministries.blogspot.com

Fig. 2   Brahmaputra River flow   Page 17

Source: Google Maps 2019

Fig. 3   Ganges Cone and Ceylon Abyssal Plain   Page 19

Source: National Geographic Maps, Indian Ocean, October 1967

Fig. 4   Initial rough plotting of Shem and Ham lands   Page 23

Source: Google Maps 2019

Fig. 5   Earth's Tectonic Plate Map   Page 25
Source:https://slideplayer.com/slide/6430925/22/images/6/Earth%E2%80%99s+Tectonic+Plates.jpg

Fig. 6   World Ocean Current Map   Page 30

Source: https://www.oceanblueproject.org/ocean-current-maps.html

Fig. 7   White and Blue Nile River   Page 33

Source: http://geography.name/nile-river/

<u>List of Figures (cont)</u>

Fig. 8   Fertile Crescent   Page 36

Source: https://www.thoughtco.com/fertile-crescent- 117266

Fig. 9   Neo-Assyrian empire ca 670 BCE   Page 36
Source:
https://irows.ucr.edu/cd/appendices/semipmarchers/semipmarcher
sapp.htm

Fig. 10 Mediterranean Sea as River Gijon   Page 39

Source: Google Maps 2019

Fig. 11 Tectonic Map showing Ham's Land   Page 41

Source:
https://slideplayer.com/slide/6430925/22/images/6/Earth%E2%80
%99s+Tectonic+Plates.jpg

Fig. 12 The Three Holy Sites   Page 43

Source: Google Maps 2019

Fig. 13 South Aegean Volcanic Arc   Page 44

Source: https://en.wikipedia.org/wiki/South_Aegean_Volcanic_Arc

List of Figures (cont)

Fig.14 Tectonic Map showing Shem's Land   Page 47

Source:

https://slideplayer.com/slide/6430925/22/images/6/Earth%E2%80

%99s+Tectonic+Plates.jpg

Fig. 15 Tectonic Convergence Lines   Page 48

Source: USGS

Fig. 16 Globe orientation after passing through Sea   Page 52

Source: Google Earth 2019

Fig. 17 Tectonic Map showing Japhet's Land   Page 55

Source:

https://slideplayer.com/slide/6430925/22/images/6/Earth%E2%80

%99s+Tectonic+Plates.jpg

Fig. 18 The Three Tongues   Page 63

Source: Google Maps 2019

About the Author

The author Cardelli has a degree in Aeronautical Science. He combines his two decades of military experience and world travels with his passion for ancient history and comparative religion to pierce the veil concealing the true nature of reality.

He is the author of "Nature of the Gods", and two upcoming books: "Reality of the Gods: A Survival Manual" currently scheduled for release in 2022, and "Dream Lord: A Lucid Dreamer's Education in Enlightenment" currently scheduled for release in 2023.

The author Cardelli resides with his wife and two sons in western Pennsylvania.

29771263R00051